# FINGERPICKING
# WORSHIP

ISBN 978-1-4234-5514-1

**HAL•LEONARD®**
CORPORATION
7777 W. BLUEMOUND RD. P.O.BOX 13819 MILWAUKEE, WI 53213

Visit Hal Leonard Online at
**www.halleonard.com**

# INTRODUCTION TO FINGERSTYLE GUITAR

Fingerstyle (a.k.a. fingerpicking) is a guitar technique that means you literally pick the strings with your right-hand fingers and thumb. This contrasts with the conventional technique of strumming and playing single notes with a pick (a.k.a. flatpicking). For fingerpicking, you can use any type of guitar: acoustic steel-string, nylon-string classical, or electric.

## THE RIGHT HAND

The most common right-hand position is shown here.

Use a high wrist; arch your palm as if you were holding a ping-pong ball. Keep the thumb outside and away from the fingers, and let the fingers do the work rather than lifting your whole hand.

The thumb generally plucks the bottom strings with downstrokes on the left side of the thumb and thumbnail. The other fingers pluck the higher strings using upstrokes with the fleshy tip of the fingers and fingernails. The thumb and fingers should pluck one string per stroke and not brush over several strings.

Another picking option you may choose to use is called hybrid picking (a.k.a. plectrum-style fingerpicking). Here, the pick is usually held between the thumb and first finger, and the three remaining fingers are assigned to pluck the higher strings.

## THE LEFT HAND

The left-hand fingers are numbered 1 through 4.

Be sure to keep your fingers arched, with each joint bent; if they flatten out across the strings, they will deaden the sound when you fingerpick. As a general rule, let the strings ring as long as possible when playing fingerstyle.

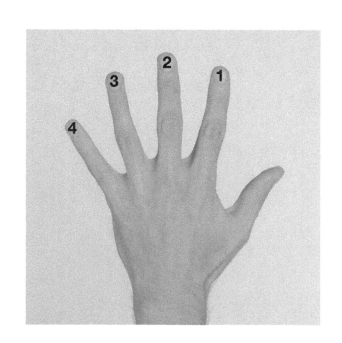

# Agnus Dei

**Words and Music by Michael W. Smith**

Drop D tuning:
(low to high) D-A-D-G-B-E

**Verse**
**Moderately**

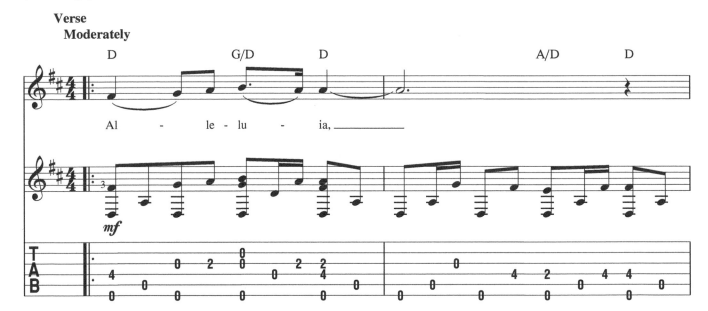

Al - le - lu - ia, ___

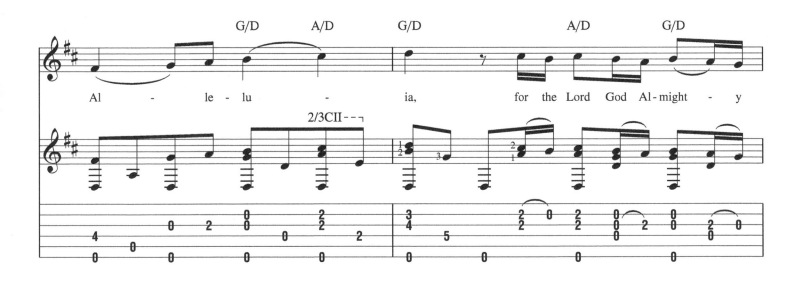

Al - le - lu - ia, ___ for the Lord God Al-might - y

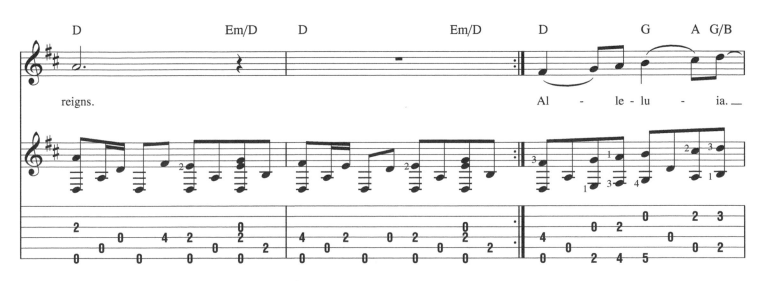

reigns. Al - le - lu - ia. ___

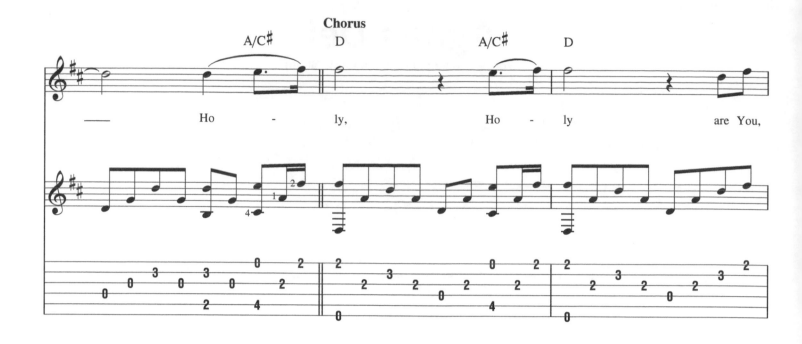

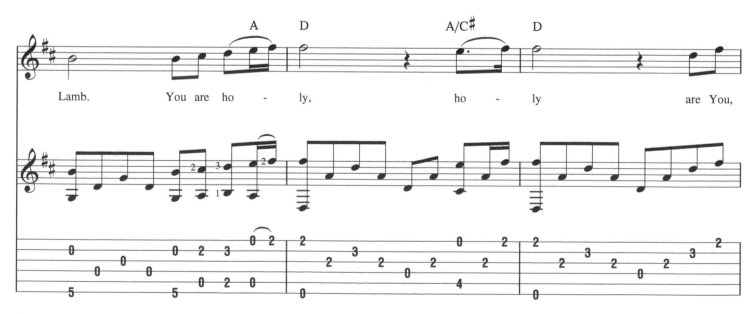

Lord God _____ Al - might - y.    Wor-thy is the Lamb,    wor-thy is the

*To Coda* ⊕                                         *D.C. al Coda*
                                                    *(take repeat)*

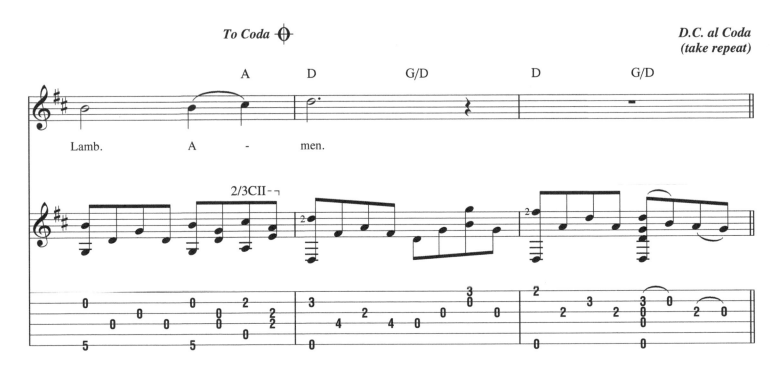

Lamb.    A -    men.

⊕ **Coda**

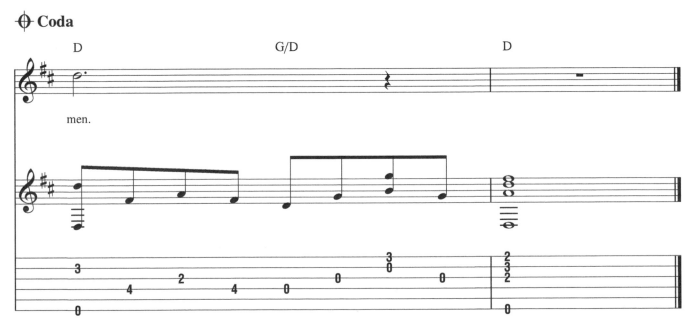

men.

# Amazing Grace
## (My Chains Are Gone)

**Words by John Newton**
**Traditional American Melody**
**Additional Words and Music by Chris Tomlin and Louie Giglio**

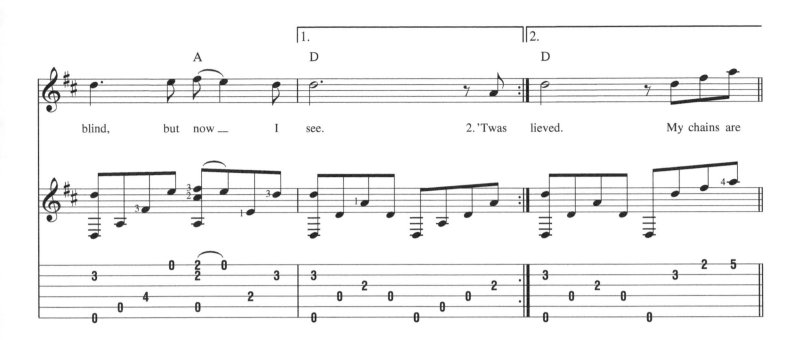

love,  a - maz -ing  grace.

3. The

⊕ **Coda**

grace.

4. The  earth  shall _ soon  dis -

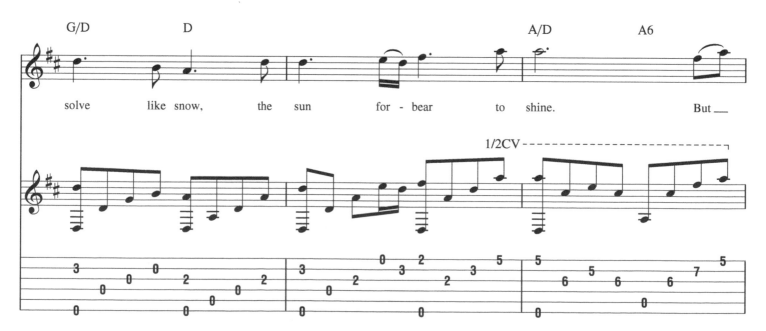

solve  like snow,  the  sun  for - bear  to  shine.  But _

1/2CV

God, who called me here be - low, will _ be for - ev - er

mine, will be for - ev - er mine.

*Additional Lyrics*

2. 'Twas grace that taught my heart to fear,
   And grace my fears relieved.
   How precious did that grace appear
   The hour I first believed.

3. The Lord has promised good to me;
   His word my hope secures.
   He will my shield and portion be,
   As long as life endures.

# Be Unto Your Name

Words and Music by Lynn DeShazo and Gary Sadler

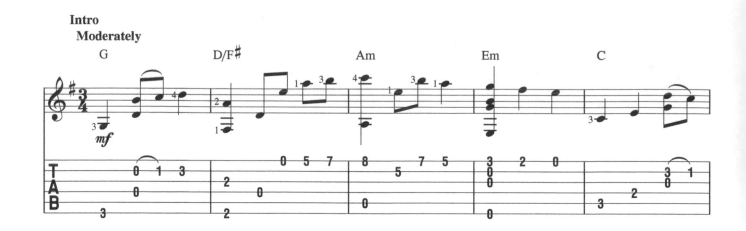

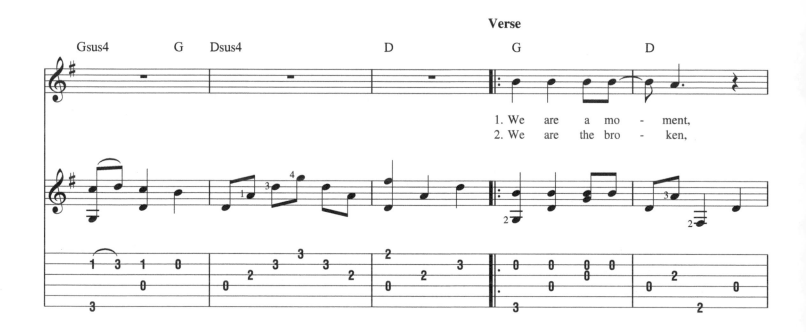

1. We are a mo - ment,
2. We are the bro - ken,

You are for - ev - er,    Lord of the ag - es,    God be - fore  

You are the heal - er,    Je - sus re - deem - er,    might - y to save.  

**Chorus**

Lamb who was slain. High - est prais - es, hon - or and glo-

-ry be un - to Your name,

be un - to Your name.

# Give Us Clean Hands

**Words and Music by Charlie Hall**

**Verse**
**Moderately**

We bow our hearts, we bend our knees. Oh, Spir - it, come make us hum-

ble. We turn our eyes from e - vil things.

**Chorus**

Oh, Lord, we cast out our i - dols. So give us clean hands ___ and give us pure hearts. ___

Let us not ___ lift our souls ___ to an-oth - er. And give us clean hands ___

___ and give us pure hearts. ___ Let us not ___ lift our souls ___ to an-oth-

- er. Oh, God, let us be ___ a gen-er-a-tion that seeks, ___ who seeks Your face, ___

oh, \_\_\_ God of Ja - cob. Oh, God, let us be \_\_\_\_\_ a gen - er - a - tion that seeks, \_\_\_

\_\_\_ who seeks Your face, \_\_\_ oh, \_\_\_ God of Ja - cob. _____

Oh, God of Ja - cob.

# Holy Spirit Rain Down

**Words and Music by Russell Fragar**

Drop D tuning:
(low to high) D-A-D-G-B-E

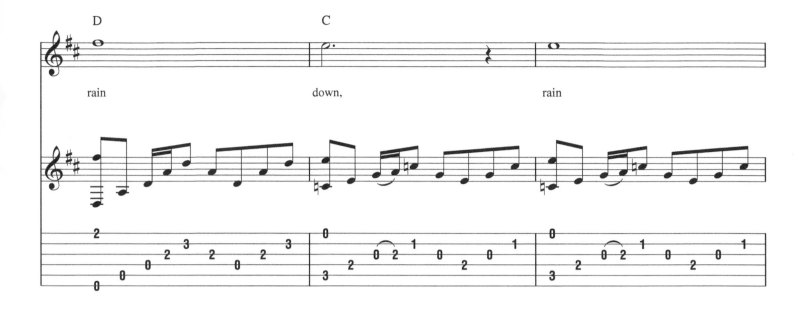

rain                    down,                   rain

down.          Let Your pow - er fall, ___ let Your voice be heard. ___ Come and

change our hearts ___ as we stand on Your word. ___ Ho - ly Spir -

G             A♯°7

o - pen up heav - en,     o - pen it wide, ____

Bm7             G/A

o - ver our church, ____     and   o - ver our lives. ____

*D.S. al Coda*           **Coda**

A                 D

____     Ho - ly Spir - it,

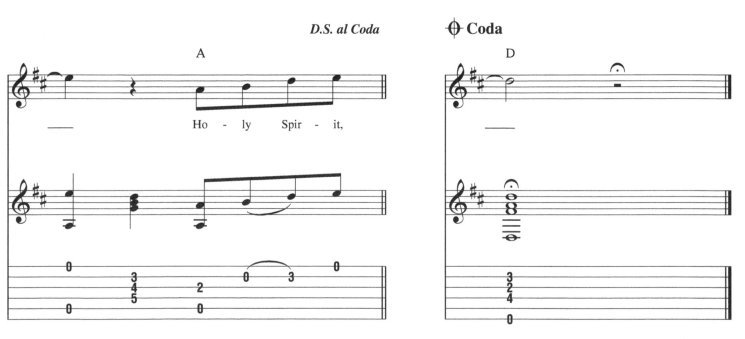

# How Deep the Father's Love for Us

**Words and Music by Stuart Townend**

Drop D tuning:
(low to high) D-A-D-G-B-E

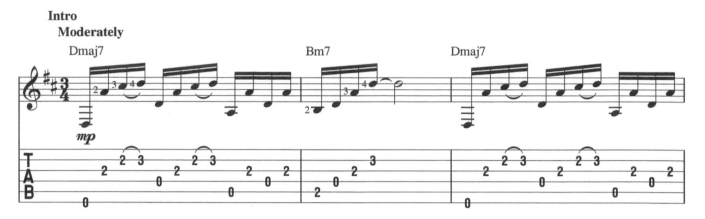

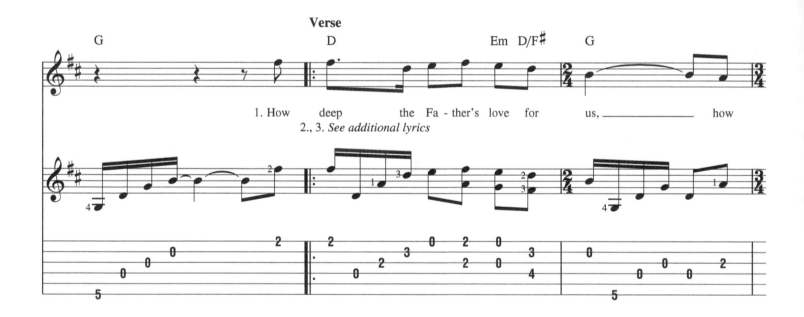

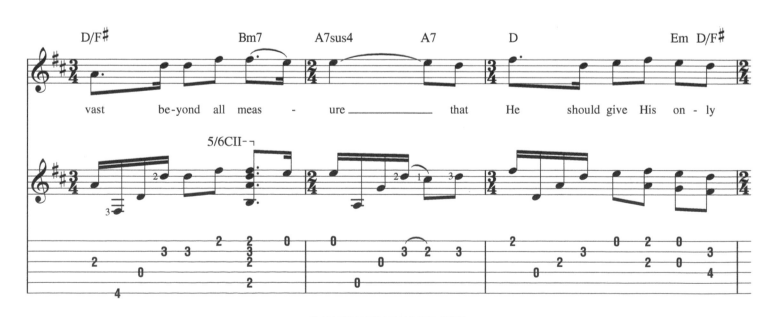

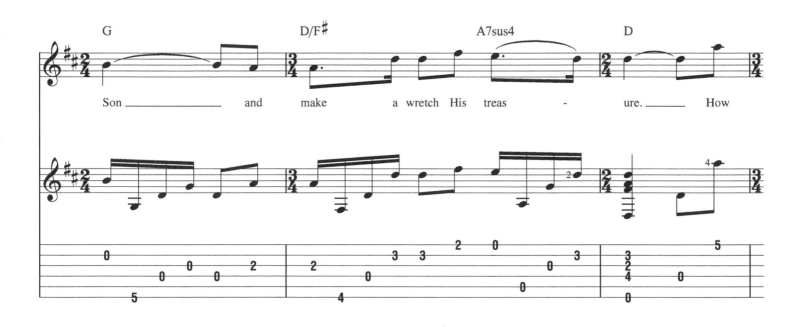

Son _____ and make a wretch His treas - ure. _____ How

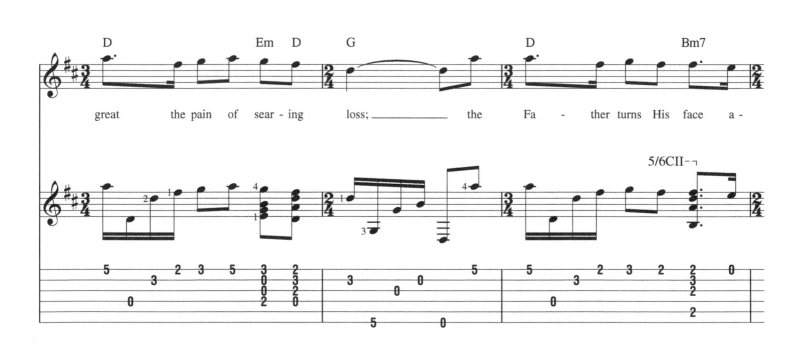

great the pain of sear - ing loss; _____ the Fa - ther turns His face a -

way _____ as wounds which mar the Cho - sen One _____ bring

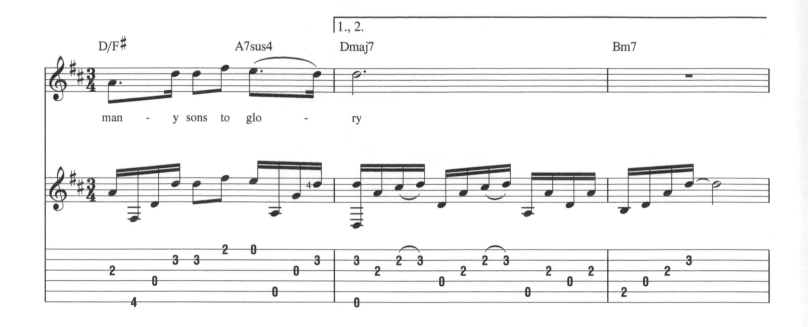

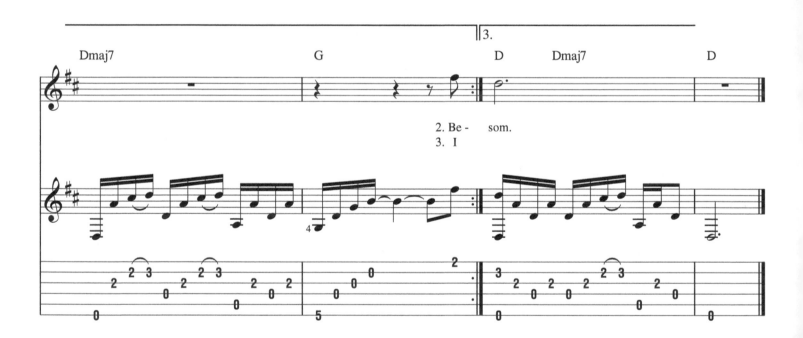

*Additional Lyrics*

2. Behold the Man upon the cross,
   My sin upon His shoulders.
   Ashamed I hear my mocking voice
   Call out among the scoffers.
   It was my sin that held Him there
   Until it was accomplished.
   His dying breath has brought me life;
   I know that it is finished.

3. I will not boast in anything;
   No gifts, no pow'r, no wisdom.
   But I will boast in Jesus Christ,
   His death and resurrection.
   Why should I gain from His reward?
   I cannot give an answer,
   But this I know with all my heart:
   His wounds have paid my ransom.

# How Great Is Our God

Words and Music by Chris Tomlin, Jesse Reeves and Ed Cash

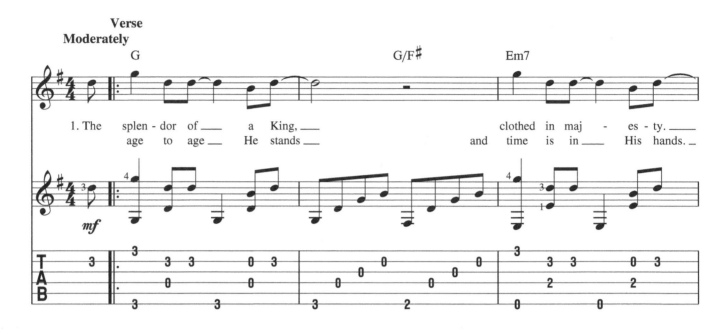

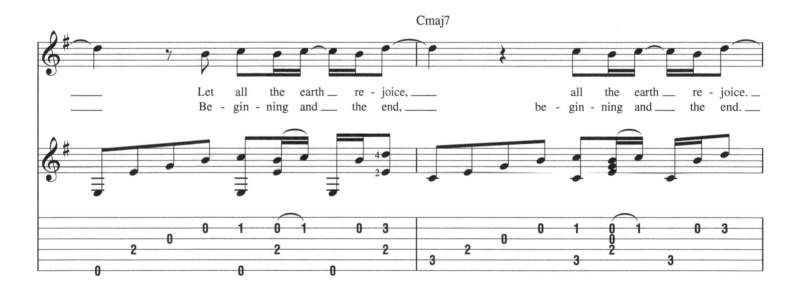

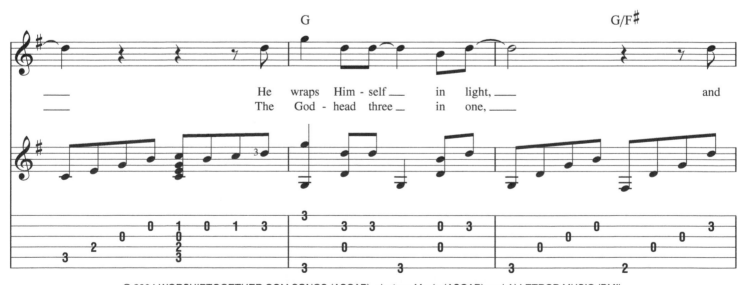

dark - ness tries _____ to hide. _____ It trem - bles at _____ His voice, _____
Fa - ther, Spir - it, Son, _____ the Li - on and _____ the Lamb, _____

_____ trem - bles at _____ His voice. _____ }
_____ Li - on and _____ the Lamb. _____ }
How great _

**Chorus**

_____ is our God! _ Sing with me: _ How great is our God! _

1/2CIII- - - - - - - - - - - - - - - - - - - - - - - - - - -

And all will see how great, how great is our

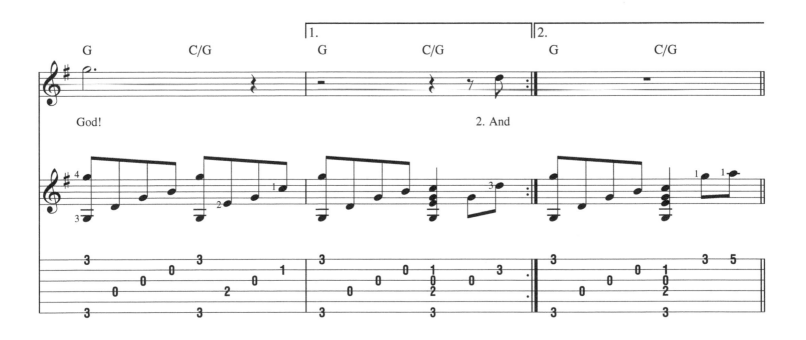

God!                                    2. And

**Bridge**

Name a - bove _____ all names, wor - thy of _____ all

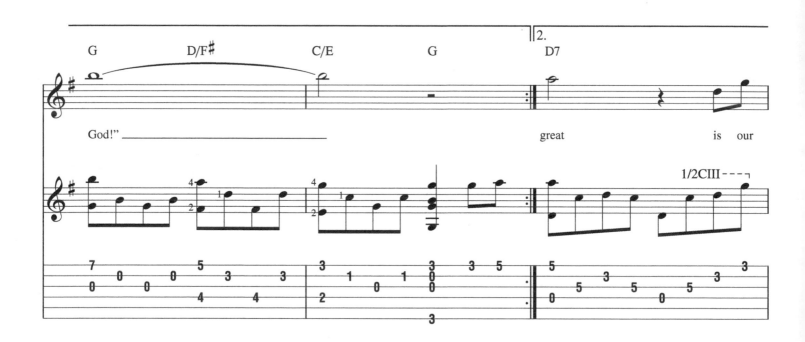

Sing with me: __ How great __ is our God! __ And all will see how

great, __ how great __ is our God!

How great __ God! _____

# I Sing Praises

**Words and Music by Terry MacAlmon**

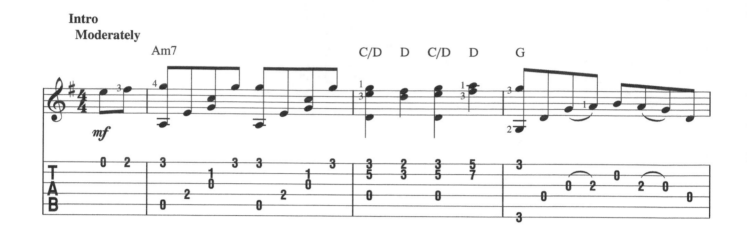

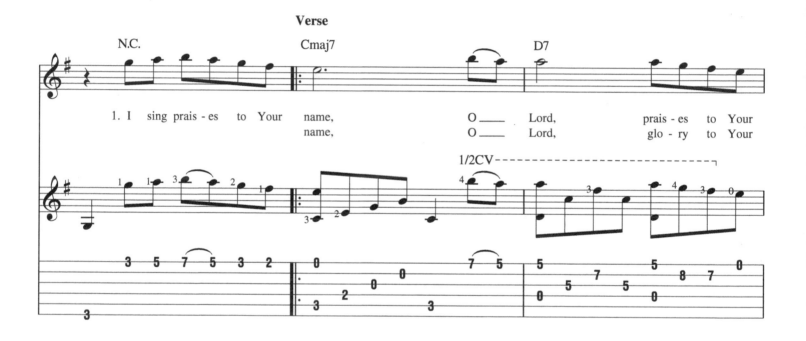

praised.

I sing prais-es to Your name, O ___ Lord, prais-es to Your
I give glo-ry to Your name, O ___ Lord, glo-ry to Your

name, O ___ Lord, for Your name is great and great-ly to be
name, O ___ Lord,

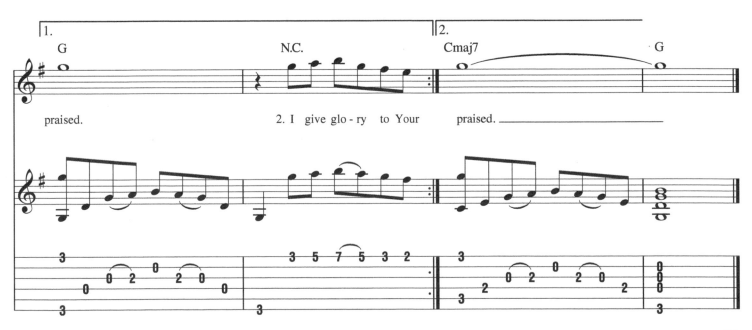

1. praised.

2. I give glo-ry to Your praised. _____

# I Worship You, Almighty God

Words and Music by Sondra Corbett-Wood

give You praise _____ for You are my right - eous - ness. _____

I wor - ship You, Al - might - y God; there is none like

You. I there is none like You. _____

# In Christ Alone

**Words and Music by Keith Getty and Stuart Townend**

Drop D tuning:
(low to high) D-A-D-G-B-E

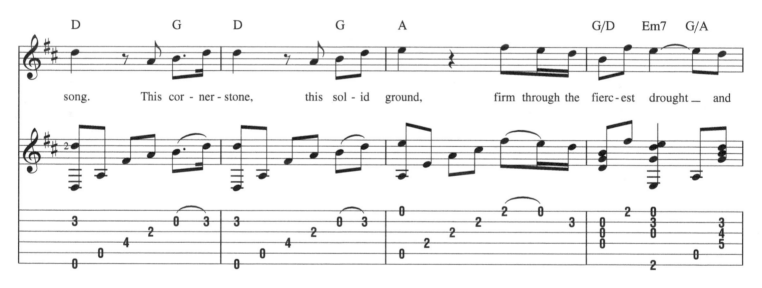

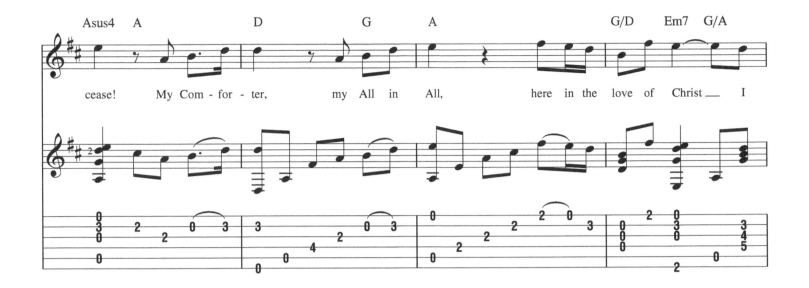

cease! My Com - for - ter, my All in All, here in the love of Christ __ I

stand.

2. In Christ a - stand. Here in the pow'r of Christ __ I'll stand.
3. There in the
4. No guilt in

*Additional Lyrics*

2. In Christ alone, who took on flesh,
   Fullness of God in helpless babe!
   This gift of love and righteousness,
   Scorned by the ones He came to save.
   Till on that cross as Jesus died,
   The wrath of God was satisfied.
   For ev'ry sin on Him was laid;
   Here in the death of Christ I live.

3. There in the ground His body lay,
   Light of the world by darkness slain.
   Then bursting forth in glorious day,
   Up from the grave He rose again!
   And as He stands in victory,
   Sin's curse has lost its grip on me.
   For I am His and He is mine;
   Bought with the precious blood of Christ.

4. No guilt in life, no fear in death,
   This is the pow'r of Christ in me.
   From life's first cry to final breath,
   Jesus commands my destiny.
   No pow'r of hell, no scheme of man,
   Can ever pluck me from His hand.
   Till He returns or calls me home;
   Here in the pow'r of Christ I'll stand.

# More Precious Than Silver

**Words and Music by Lynn DeShazo**

Drop D tuning:
(low to high) D-A-D-G-B-E

**Verse**
**Moderately**

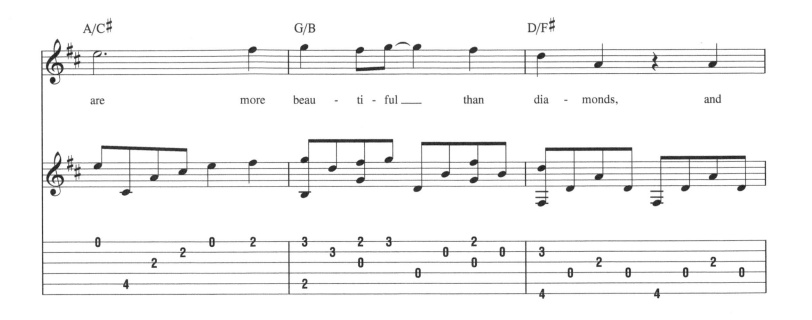

are     more   beau - ti - ful \_\_\_ than   dia - monds,     and

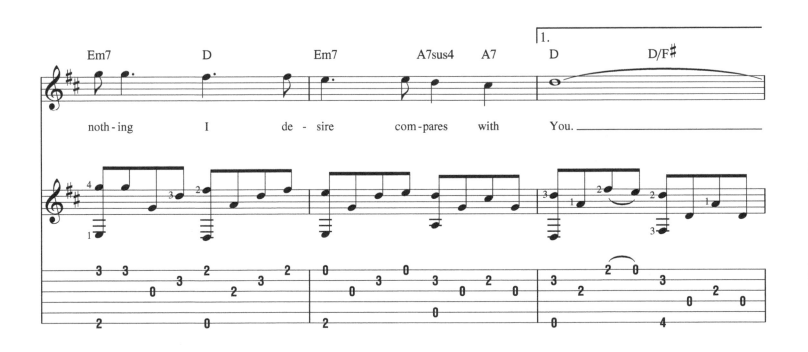

noth - ing    I    de - sire   com - pares   with    You. _____

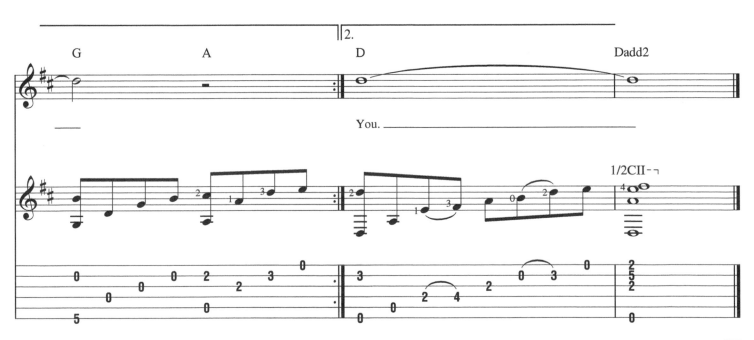

\_\_\_            You. _____

# Offering

**Words and Music by Paul Baloche**

**Verse**
**Moderately slow**

The sun __ can-not __ com - pare __ to the glo - ry of __ Your love. __

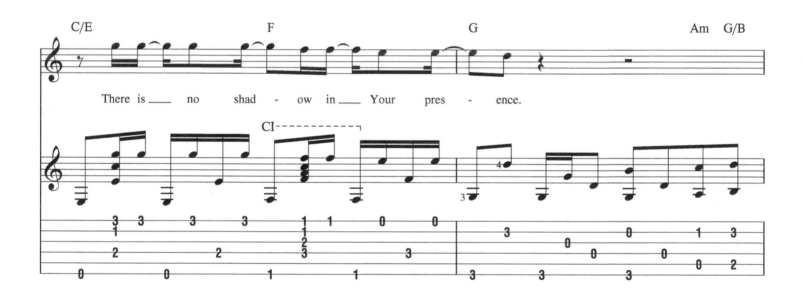

There is __ no shad - ow in __ Your pres - ence.

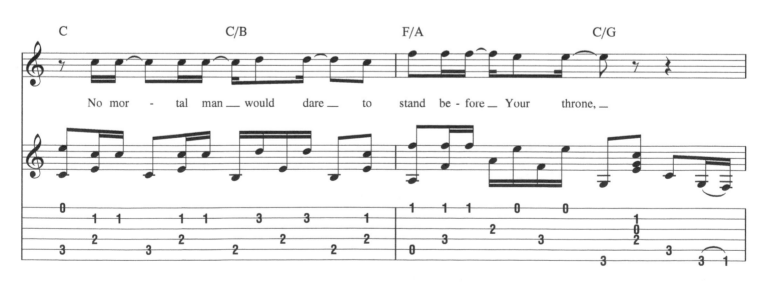

No mor - tal man __ would dare __ to stand be - fore __ Your throne, __

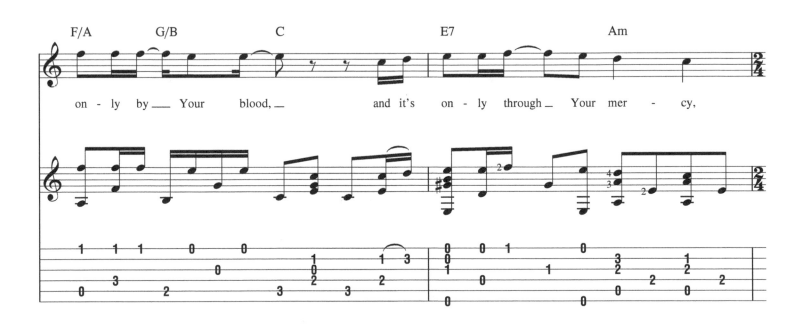

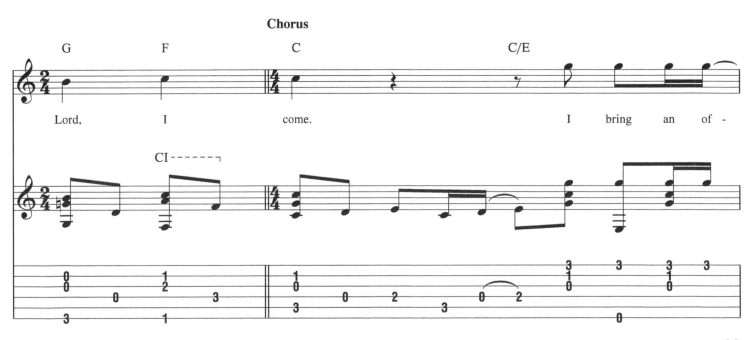

-fer - ing __ of wor - ship to __ my King. No one on earth __

__ de - serves __ the prais - es that __ I sing. Je - sus, may You __

__ re - cieve __ the hon - or that You're __ due. O

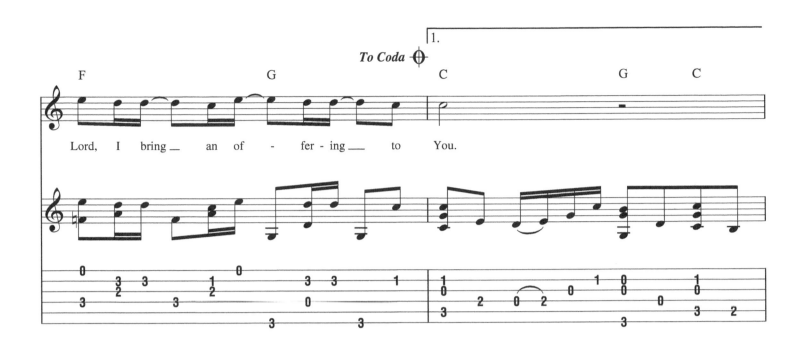

Lord, I bring __ an of - fer - ing __ to You.

I bring an of - fer - ing __ to You.

You.    I bring an of -

**Coda**

You.

O Lord, ___ I bring ___ an of - fer - ing ___ to

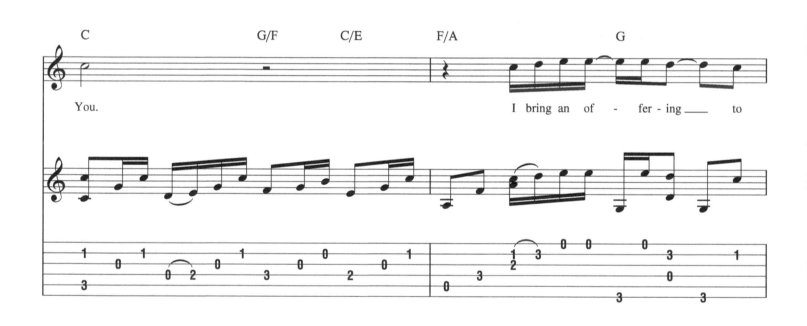

You.

I bring an of - fer - ing ___ to

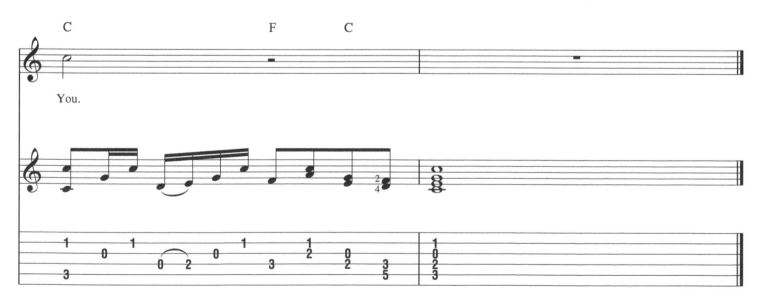

You.

# There Is a Redeemer

**Words and Music by Melody Green**

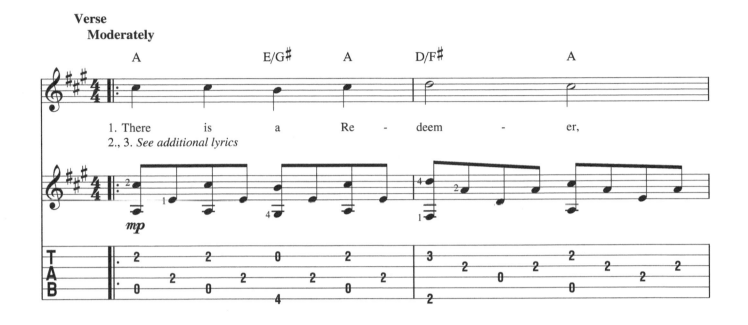

1. There is a Re - deem - er,
2., 3. *See additional lyrics*

Je - sus, God's own Son. _____ Pre - cious Lamb of

God, Mes - si - ah, Ho - ly One.

**Chorus**

slain.
place.

Thank You, oh, my Fa - ther, for

giv - ing us ___ Your Son, _____ and leav - ing Your

*To Coda* ⊕

*D.C. al Coda*
*(take 2nd ending)*

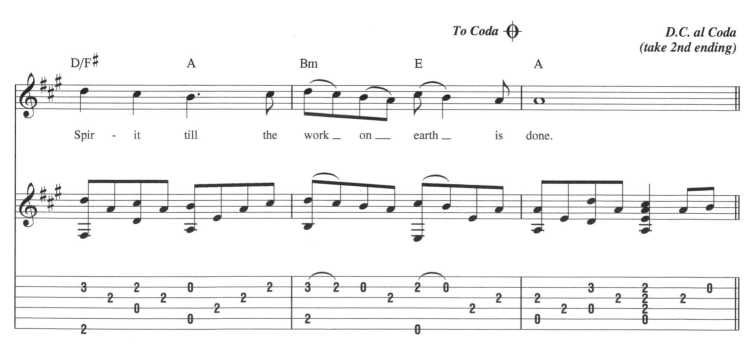

Spir - it till the work __ on __ earth __ is done.

**Coda**

Verse

**Chorus**

One.      Thank You,   oh,   my   Fa - ther,   for

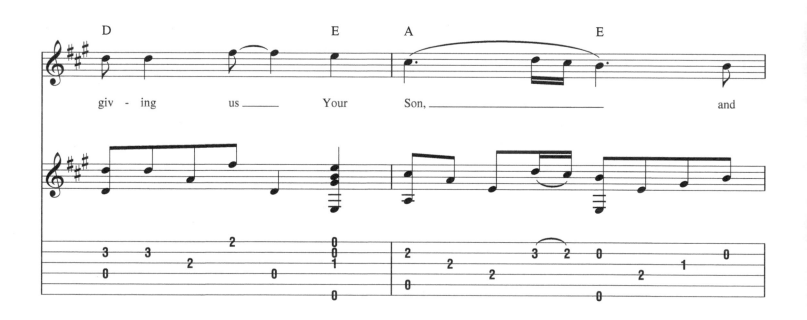

giv - ing     us \_\_\_\_   Your   Son, _____    and

leav - ing   Your   Spir - it   till   the   work \_ on \_ earth \_ is

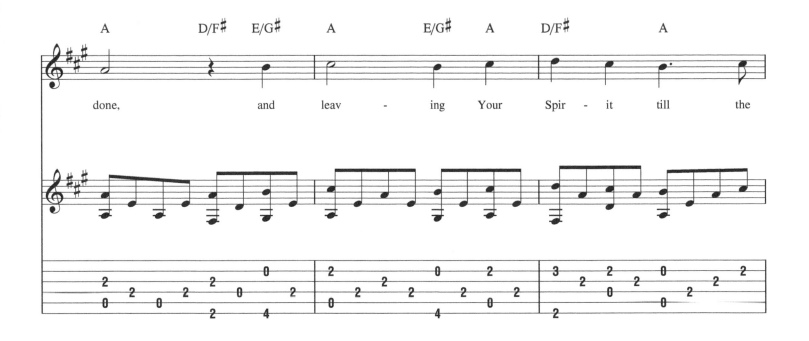

done, and leav - ing Your Spir - it till the

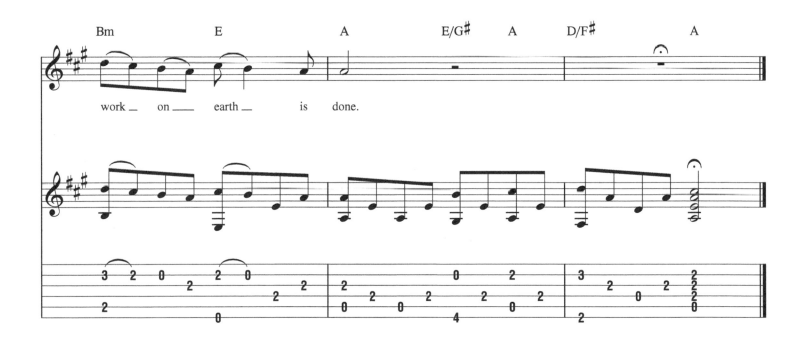

work on earth is done.

*Additional Lyrics*

2. Jesus, my Redeemer,
   Name above all names,
   Precious Lamb of God, Messiah,
   Oh, for sinners slain.

3. When I stand in glory,
   I will see His face,
   And there I'll serve my King forever
   In that holy place.

# We Fall Down

**Words and Music by Chris Tomlin**

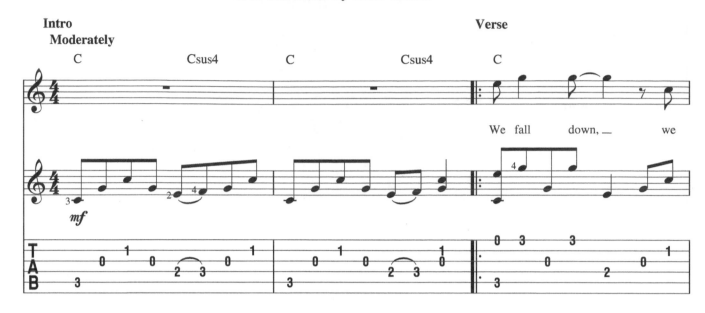

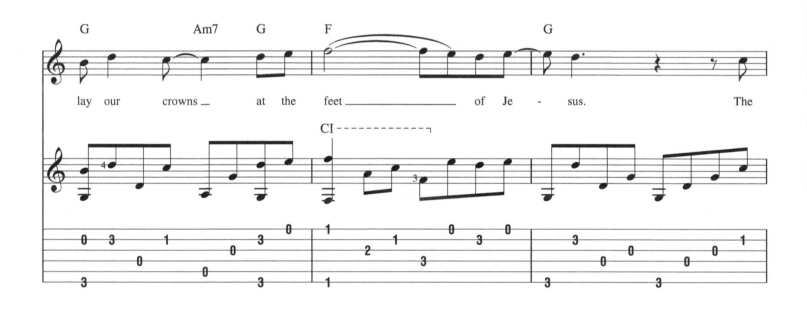

**Chorus**

"Ho - ly, ho - ly, ho - ly." We cry, "Ho - ly, ho - ly, ho - ly." We cry,

"Ho - ly, ho - ly, ho - ly is the Lamb."

**Outro**

"Ho - ly, ho - ly, ho - ly is the Lamb."

# The Wonderful Cross

**Words and Music by Jesse Reeves, Chris Tomlin and J.D. Walt**

Intro
Moderately

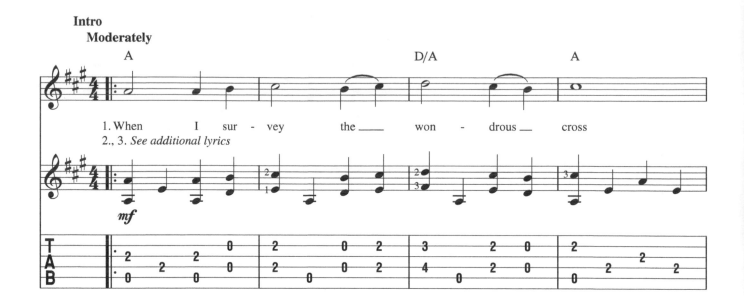

1. When I sur - vey the won - drous cross
2., 3. *See additional lyrics*

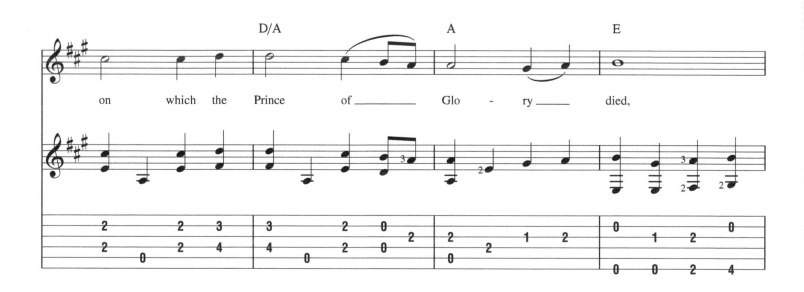

on which the Prince of Glo - ry died,

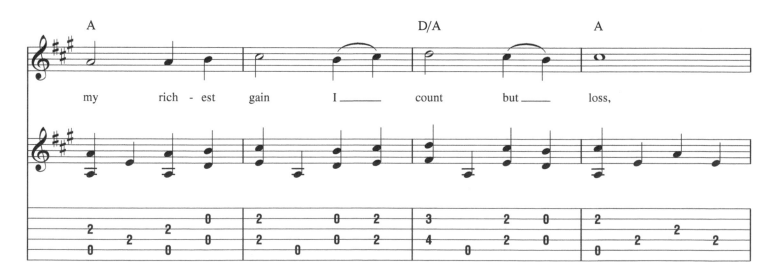

my rich - est gain I count but loss,

and pour con - tempt on all my _____ pride.

**Chorus**

crown?⎫
all. ⎬

O the won - der - ful cross, _____ O the

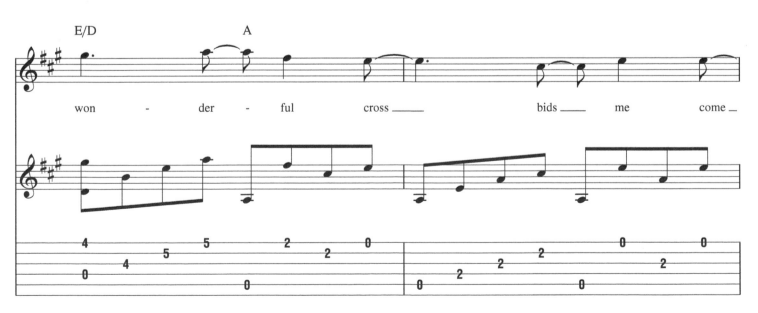

won - der - ful cross _____ bids _____ me come _

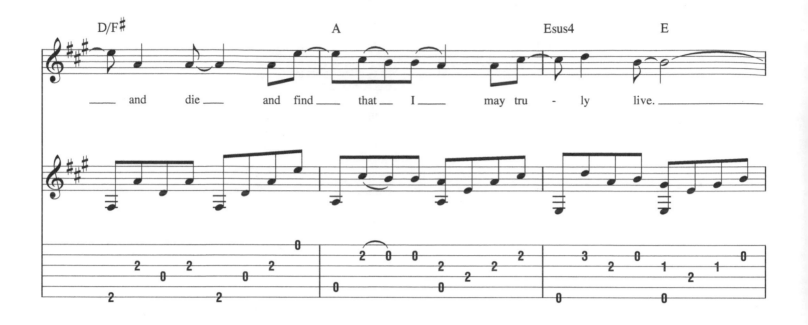

and die __ and find __ that __ I __ may tru - ly live. __

__ O the won - der - ful cross, __ O the

won - der - ful cross, __ all __ who gath - er here __ by grace __

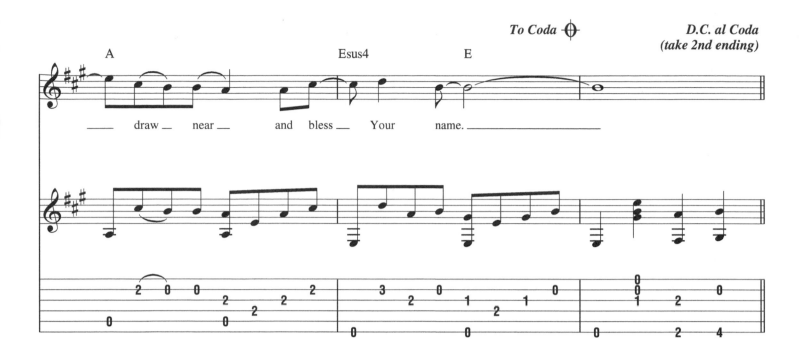

draw — near — and bless — Your name. _____

⊕ **Coda**

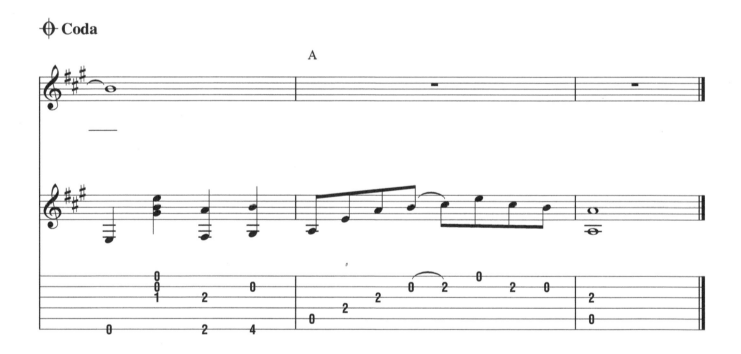

*Additional Lyrics*

2. See from His head, His hands, His feet
   Sorrow and love flow mingled down.
   Did ever such love and sorrow meet,
   Or thorns compose so rich a crown?

3. Were the whole realm of nature mine,
   That were an offering far too small.
   Love so amazing, so divine,
   Demands my soul, my life, my all.

# FINGERPICKING GUITAR BOOKS

*Hone your fingerpicking skills with these great songbooks featuring solo guitar arrangements in standard notation and tablature. The arrangements in these books are carefully written for intermediate-level guitarists. Each song combines melody and harmony in one superb guitar fingerpicking arrangement. Each book also includes an introduction to basic fingerstyle guitar.*

**Fingerpicking Acoustic**
00699614  15 songs......................$14.99

**Fingerpicking Acoustic Classics**
00160211  15 songs......................$16.99

**Fingerpicking Acoustic Hits**
00160202  15 songs......................$12.99

**Fingerpicking Acoustic Rock**
00699764  14 songs......................$16.99

**Fingerpicking Ballads**
00699717  15 songs......................$14.99

**Fingerpicking Beatles**
00699049  30 songs......................$24.99

**Fingerpicking Beethoven**
00702390  15 pieces......................$10.99

**Fingerpicking Blues**
00701277  15 songs......................$10.99

**Fingerpicking
Broadway Favorites**
00699843  15 songs......................$9.99

**Fingerpicking Broadway Hits**
00699838  15 songs......................$7.99

**Fingerpicking Campfire**
00275964  15 songs......................$12.99

**Fingerpicking Celtic Folk**
00701148  15 songs......................$12.99

**Fingerpicking Children's Songs**
00699712  15 songs......................$9.99

**Fingerpicking Christian**
00701076  15 songs......................$12.99

**Fingerpicking Christmas**
00699599  20 carols......................$10.99

**Fingerpicking
Christmas Classics**
00701695  15 songs......................$7.99

**Fingerpicking Christmas Songs**
00171333  15 songs......................$10.99

**Fingerpicking Classical**
00699620  15 pieces......................$10.99

**Fingerpicking Country**
00699687  17 songs......................$12.99

**Fingerpicking Disney**
00699711  15 songs......................$16.99

**Fingerpicking
Early Jazz Standards**
00276565  15 songs ......................$12.99

**Fingerpicking Duke Ellington**
00699845  15 songs......................$9.99

**Fingerpicking Enya**
00701161  15 songs......................$16.99

**Fingerpicking Film Score Music**
00160143  15 songs......................$12.99

**Fingerpicking Gospel**
00701059  15 songs......................$9.99

**Fingerpicking Hit Songs**
00160195  15 songs......................$12.99

**Fingerpicking Hymns**
00699688  15 hymns ......................$12.99

**Fingerpicking Irish Songs**
00701965  15 songs......................$10.99

**Fingerpicking Italian Songs**
00159778  15 songs......................$12.99

**Fingerpicking Jazz Favorites**
00699844  15 songs......................$12.99

**Fingerpicking Jazz Standards**
00699840  15 songs......................$12.99

**Fingerpicking Elton John**
00237495  15 songs......................$14.99

**Fingerpicking Latin Favorites**
00699842  15 songs......................$12.99

**Fingerpicking Latin Standards**
00699837  15 songs......................$17.99

**Fingerpicking
Andrew Lloyd Webber**
00699839  14 songs......................$16.99

**Fingerpicking Love Songs**
00699841  15 songs......................$14.99

**Fingerpicking Love Standards**
00699836  15 songs ......................$9.99

**Fingerpicking Lullabyes**
00701276  16 songs......................$9.99

**Fingerpicking Movie Music**
00699919  15 songs......................$14.99

**Fingerpicking Mozart**
00699794  15 pieces......................$10.99

**Fingerpicking Pop**
00699615  15 songs......................$14.99

**Fingerpicking Popular Hits**
00139079  14 songs......................$12.99

**Fingerpicking Praise**
00699714  15 songs......................$14.99

**Fingerpicking Rock**
00699716  15 songs......................$14.99

**Fingerpicking Standards**
00699613  17 songs......................$14.99

**Fingerpicking Wedding**
00699637  15 songs......................$10.99

**Fingerpicking Worship**
00700554  15 songs......................$14.99

**Fingerpicking Neil Young –
Greatest Hits**
00700134  16 songs......................$16.99

**Fingerpicking Yuletide**
00699654  16 songs......................$12.99

**HAL•LEONARD®**

Order these and more great publications from your
favorite music retailer at
**halleonard.com**

*Prices, contents and availability
subject to change without notice.*

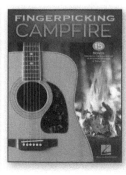
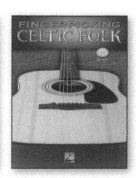

# AUTHENTIC CHORDS • ORIGINAL KEYS • COMPLETE SONGS

The *Strum It* series lets players strum the chords and sing along with their favorite hits. Each song has been selected because it can be played with regular open chords, barre chords, or other moveable chord types. Guitarists can simply play the rhythm, or play and sing along through the entire song. All songs are shown in their original keys complete with chords, strum patterns, melody and lyrics. Wherever possible, the chord voicings from the recorded versions are notated.

**THE BEACH BOYS' GREATEST HITS**
00699357......................................$12.95

**THE BEATLES FAVORITES**
00699249.........................................$15.99

**VERY BEST OF JOHNNY CASH**
00699514.........................................$14.99

**CELTIC GUITAR SONGBOOK**
00699265.........................................$12.99

**CHRISTMAS SONGS FOR GUITAR**
00699247.........................................$10.95

**CHRISTMAS SONGS WITH 3 CHORDS**
00699487...........................................$9.99

**VERY BEST OF ERIC CLAPTON**
00699560.........................................$12.95

**JIM CROCE – CLASSIC HITS**
00699269.........................................$10.95

**DISNEY FAVORITES**
00699171.........................................$14.99

**MELISSA ETHERIDGE GREATEST HITS**
00699518.........................................$12.99

**FAVORITE SONGS WITH 3 CHORDS**
00699112.........................................$10.99

**FAVORITE SONGS WITH 4 CHORDS**
00699270...........................................$8.95

**FIRESIDE SING-ALONG**
00699273.........................................$12.99

**FOLK FAVORITES**
00699517...........................................$8.95

**THE GUITAR STRUMMERS' ROCK SONGBOOK**
00701678.........................................$14.99

**BEST OF WOODY GUTHRIE**
00699496.........................................$12.95

**JOHN HIATT COLLECTION**
00699398.........................................$17.99

**THE VERY BEST OF BOB MARLEY**
00699524.........................................$14.99

**A MERRY CHRISTMAS SONGBOOK**
00699211.........................................$10.99

**MORE FAVORITE SONGS WITH 3 CHORDS**
00699532...........................................$9.99

**THE VERY BEST OF TOM PETTY**
00699336.........................................$15.99

**BEST OF GEORGE STRAIT**
00699235.........................................$16.99

**TAYLOR SWIFT FOR ACOUSTIC GUITAR**
00109717.........................................$16.99

**BEST OF HANK WILLIAMS JR.**
00699224.........................................$16.99

Prices, contents & availability
subject to change without notice.

Visit Hal Leonard online at
**www.halleonard.com**

# christian guitar songbooks

*from* **Hal•Leonard®**

## ACOUSTIC GUITAR WORSHIP

30 praise song favorites arranged for guitar, including: Awesome God • Forever • I Could Sing of Your Love Forever • Lord, Reign in Me • Open the Eyes of My Heart • and more.

00699672 Solo Guitar .......................................... $14.99

## FAVORITE HYMNS FOR SOLO GUITAR

Amazing Grace • Christ the Lord Is Risen Today • For the Beauty of the Earth • Holy, Holy, Holy • In the Garden • Let Us Break Bread Together • O for a Thousand Tongues to Sing • Were You There? • What a Friend We Have in Jesus • When I Survey the Wondrous Cross • more.

00699275 Fingerstyle Guitar ................................ $12.99

## FINGERPICKING HYMNS

Abide with Me • Amazing Grace • Beneath the Cross of Jesus • Come, Thou Fount of Every Blessing • For the Beauty of the Earth • A Mighty Fortress Is Our God • Rock of Ages • and more.

00699688 Solo Guitar .............................................. $9.99

## FINGERPICKING WORSHIP

Agnus Dei • Amazing Grace (My Chains Are Gone) • How Deep the Father's Love for Us • How Great Is Our God • I Worship You, Almighty God • More Precious Than Silver • There Is a Redeemer • We Fall Down • and more, plus an easy introduction to basic fingerstyle guitar.

00700554 Solo Guitar .......................................... $10.99

## GOSPEL GUITAR SONGBOOK

Includes notes & tab for fingerpicking and Travis picking arrangements of 15 favorites: Amazing Grace • Blessed Assurance • Do Lord • I've Got Peace Like a River • Just a Closer Walk with Thee • O Happy Day • Precious Memories • Rock of Ages • Swing Low, Sweet Chariot • There Is Power in the Blood • When the Saints Go Marching In and more!

00695372 Guitar with Notes & Tab ........................ $9.95

## GOSPEL HYMNS

Amazing Grace • At the Cross • Blessed Assurance • Higher Ground • I've Got Peace like a River • In the Garden • Love Lifted Me • The Old Rugged Cross • Rock of Ages • What a Friend We Have in Jesus • When the Saints Go Marching In • Wondrous Love • and more.

00700463
Lyrics/Chord Symbols/Guitar Chord Diagrams........ $14.99

## HYMNS FOR CLASSICAL GUITAR

Amazing Grace • Be Thou My Vision • Come, Thou Fount of Every Blessing • For the Beauty of the Earth • Joyful, Joyful, We Adore Thee • My Faith Looks up to Thee • Rock of Ages • What a Friend We Have in Jesus • and more.

00701898 Solo Guitar .......................................... $14.99

## HYMNS FOR SOLO JAZZ GUITAR

*Book/Online Video*

Abide with Me • Amazing Grace • Blessed Assurance • God Is So Good • Just a Closer Walk with Thee • Londonderry Air • Oh How I Love Jesus • Softly and Tenderly • Sweet Hour of Prayer • What a Friend We Have in Jesus.

00153842 Solo Guitar .......................................... $19.99

## MODERN WORSHIP – GUITAR CHORD SONGBOOK

Amazed • Amazing Grace (My Chains Are Gone) • At the Cross • Beautiful One • Everlasting God • How Can I Keep from Singing • I Am Free • Let God Arise • Let My Words Be Few (I'll Stand in Awe of You) • Made to Worship • Mighty to Save • Nothing but the Blood • Offering • Sing to the King • Today Is the Day • Your Name • and more.

00701801
Lyrics/Chord Symbols/Guitar Chord Diagrams........ $16.99

## PRAISE & WORSHIP – STRUM & SING

This inspirational collection features 25 favorites for guitarists to strum and sing. Includes chords and lyrics for: Amazing Grace (My Chains Are Gone) • Cornerstone • Everlasting God • Forever • The Heart of Worship • How Great Is Our God • In Christ Alone • Mighty to Save • 10,000 Reasons (Bless the Lord) • This I Believe • We Fall Down • and more.

00152381 Guitar/Vocal .......................................... $12.99

## SACRED SONGS FOR CLASSICAL GUITAR

Bind Us Together • El Shaddai • Here I Am, Lord • His Name Is Wonderful • How Great Thou Art • I Walked Today Where Jesus Walked • On Eagle's Wings • Thou Art Worthy • and more.

00702426 Guitar ................................................. $14.99

## SUNDAY SOLOS FOR GUITAR

Great Is Thy Faithfulness • Here I Am to Worship • How Great Is Our God • Joyful, Joyful, We Adore Thee • There Is a Redeemer • We Fall Down • What a Friend We Have in Jesus • and more!

00703083 Guitar ................................................. $14.99

## TOP CHRISTIAN HITS – STRUM & SING GUITAR

Good Good Father (Chris Tomlin) • Greater (MercyMe) • Holy Spirit (Francesca Battistelli) • I Am (Crowder) • Same Power (Jeremy Camp) • This Is Amazing Grace (Phil Wickham) • and more.

00156331 Guitar/Vocal .......................................... $12.99

## THE WORSHIP GUITAR ANTHOLOGY – VOLUME 1

This collection contains melody, lyrics & chords for 100 contemporary favorites, such as: Beautiful One • Forever • Here I Am to Worship • Hosanna (Praise Is Rising) • How He Loves • In Christ Alone • Mighty to Save • Our God • Revelation Song • Your Grace Is Enough • and dozens more.

00101864 Melody/Lyrics/Chords........................... $16.99

## WORSHIP SOLOS FOR FINGERSTYLE GUITAR

Ancient Words • Before the Throne of God Above • Broken Vessels (Amazing Grace) • Cornerstone • Good Good Father • Great Are You Lord • Holy Spirit • I Will Rise • King of My Heart • Lord, I Need You • O Come to the Altar • O Praise the Name (Anastasis) • Oceans (Where Feet May Fail) • 10,000 Reasons (Bless the Lord) • Your Name.

00276831 Guitar .................................................. $14.99

## TOP WORSHIP SONGS FOR GUITAR

Amazing Grace (My Chains Are Gone) • Because He Lives, Amen • Cornerstone • Forever (We Sing Hallelujah) • Good Good Father • Holy Spirit • Jesus Messiah • Lead Me to the Cross • Our God • Revelation Song • This Is Amazing Grace • We Believe • Your Grace Is Enough • and more.

00160854 Melody/Lyrics/Chords........................... $12.99

*Prices, contents and availability subject to change without notice.*

**FOR MORE INFORMATION, SEE YOUR LOCAL MUSIC DEALER, OR WRITE TO:**

**HAL•LEONARD®**

7777 W. BLUEMOUND RD. P.O. BOX 13819
MILWAUKEE, WISCONSIN 53213

www.halleonard.com